S0-AJD-489

WORLD CULTURES

Living in the
Amazon Rain Forest

Anita Ganeri

Raintree

Chicago, Illinois

© 2008 Raintree
Published by Raintree,
a division of Reed Elsevier Inc.
Chicago, Illinois

Customer Service   888–454–2279

Visit our website at www.heinemannraintree.com

All rights reserved. No part of this publication may be
reproduced or transmitted in any form or by any means,
electronic or mechanical, including photocopying,
recording, taping, or any information storage and
retrieval system, without permission in writing from
the publisher.

Designed by Richard Parker and Manhattan Design
Printed and bound in China by SCPC

12 11 10 09 08
10 9 8 7 6 5 4 3 2 1

Library of Congress Cataloging-in-Publication Data
Ganeri, Anita, 1961.
Living in the Amazon rain forest.
p. cm. -- (World cultures)
Includes bibliographical references and index.
ISBN-13: 978-1-4109-2817-7 (library binding–hardcover)
ISBN-10: 1-4109-2817-9 (library binding–hardcover)
ISBN-13: 978-1-4109-2826-9 (pbk.)
ISBN-10: 1-4109-2826-8 (pbk.)
1. Yanomami Indians--Social life and customs--Juvenile
literature. 2. Rain forests--Brazil--Juvenile literature.
3. Rain forests--Venezuela--Juvenile literature. 4. Brazil--
Social life and customs--Juvenile literature. 5. Venezuela-
Social life and customs--Juvenile literature.
I. Title.
F2520.1.Y3G36 2007
981'.130049892--dc22
                          2007003278

Acknowledgments
The publishers would like to thank the following for
permission to reproduce photographs: Alamy Images
pp. **16** (Sue Cunningham Photographic), **29** (James
Quine); Art Directors and Trip/ Bob Masters pp. **9, 14, 15,
21**; Corbis pp. **20** (Owen Franken), **22** (Tom Brakefield),
25 (Sygma), **28** (Royalty Free); Digital Vision pp. **7, 18**;
FLPA/ Tui De Roy/ Minden Pictures p. **6**; Getty Images/
Time Life Pictures p. **13**; Getty Images (Victor Englebert/
Time & Life Pictures) pp. **4, 8, 19, 23**; NHPA pp. **17** (Martin
Harvey), **12** (Ross Nolly); Panos Pictures/ Jerry Callow
p. **24**; Rex Features pp. **10** (Action Press), **27** (Sipa Press);
Still Pictures/ Mark Edwards pp. **11, 26**.

Illustrations by International Mapping.

Cover photograph of a Yanomami man in Brazil made
up for a feast, reproduced with permission of Robert
Harding/ Robin Tenison.

Every effort has been made to contact copyright holders
of any material reproduced in this book. Any omissions
will be rectified in subsequent printings if notice is given
to the publishers.

Contents

Some words are printed in bold, **like this**. You can find out what they mean on page 31.

The Yanomami

The Yanomami are a group of people who live in South America. The name "Yanomami" means "human being." There are over 20,000 Yanomami. About half of the Yanomami population lives in the country of Brazil. The other half lives in Venezuela (see map on page 5). The Yanomami live in thick, green **rain forest**.

◀ A group of Yanomami men takes shelter from the rain underneath a banana leaf in the Amazon rain forest.

The Yanomami live in the Amazon rain forest. This is the biggest rain forest in the world. The huge Amazon River runs through it. The rain forest covers an area of about 2.3 million square miles (6 million square kilometers). It is almost the size of Australia, or 10 times the size of Texas.

The first Yanomami

The Yanomami have lived in the rain forest for thousands of years. Long ago, the first Yanomami traveled from Asia to North America (see smaller map below). Then, they headed south to South America. Gradually, they moved closer and closer to the Amazon River.

▲ This map shows where the Yanomami live in the Amazon rain forest. Their lands are split between the countries of Brazil and Venezuela.

Life in the Forest

The Yanomami live deep inside the **rain forest**. They call the rain forest *Urihi*. *Urihi* means "forest land." Everything they need comes from the rain forest.

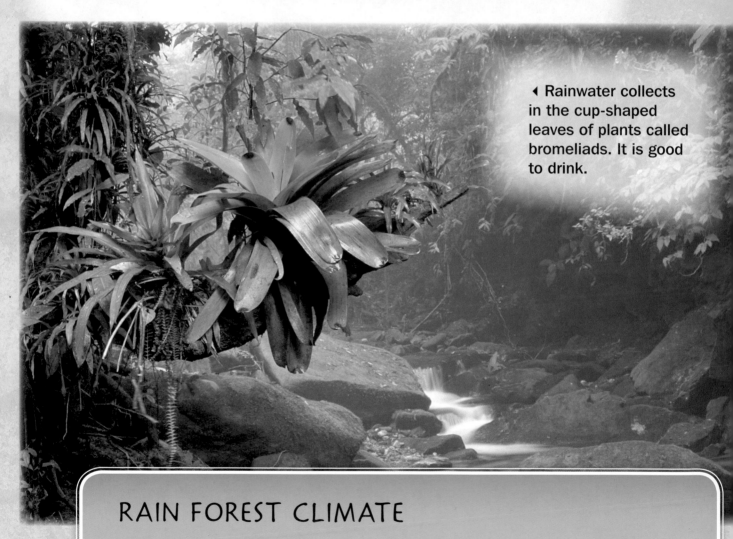

◄ Rainwater collects in the cup-shaped leaves of plants called bromeliads. It is good to drink.

RAIN FOREST CLIMATE

The **equator** runs through the Amazon rain forest. The equator is an imaginary line around Earth. The rain forest **climate** is always hot and steamy. In the wet season, it rains heavily on most days. It rains less in the dry season, but it can still be very wet. The heat and damp are ideal conditions for plants to grow all year round.

Survival skills

The Yanomami have learned special skills for surviving. They know which rain forest plants are good for food and medicine. They know which plants are good for building materials. They know which rain forest animals to hunt for food. The Yanomami share the forest with the plants and animals. They treat it very carefully and with respect.

▶ A brightly colored bird called a toucan perches on the branch of a rain forest tree. Yanomami children sometimes keep toucans as pets.

Life in the Community

The Yanomami live in hundreds of small villages. These are scattered widely across the **rain forest**. Between 40 and 150 people live in each village.

Everyone in the village has a job. Some people help build houses or go hunting. Others grow fruits and vegetables. Today, some villagers trade with people from other **cultures**. These people give the Yanomami factory-made goods, such as metal cooking pots or wristwatches.

◀ Yanomami women carry baskets of manioc (see page 15), which they have been gathering in the forest.

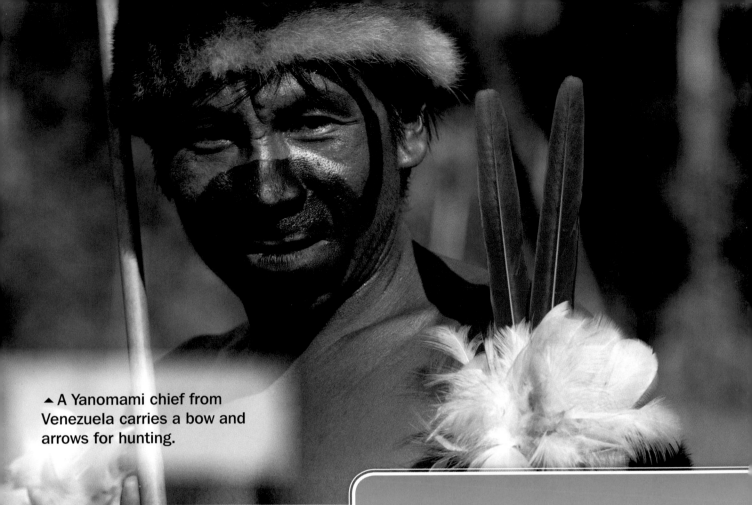

▲ A Yanomami chief from Venezuela carries a bow and arrows for hunting.

Village visiting

Each village has a leader, or chief. The chief looks after the village. He is in charge of activities such as building a new house. Other villagers can come to the chief for advice. The Yanomami regularly travel through the forest to other villages. They visit friends and relatives. They also attend feasts and other celebrations.

YANOMAMI LANGUAGES

The Yanomami speak different languages, depending on where they live. The languages are quite similar. People often understand each other even when their language is slightly different. Here are some words and phrases to try out:

Awe	(Aw-eh)	Yes
Ma	(Mah)	No
Ara	(Ah-rah)	Macaw (large parrot)
Waka	(Wah-kah)	Armadillo (mammal)
Iro	(Ee-roh)	Howler monkeys
Oshe	(Osh-eh)	Termites (insects)

A Yanomami House

In many Yanomami villages, everyone lives together in one big, round hut. The hut is called a **yano**. There is a large open space in the middle of the *yano*. This is where Yanomami children play. Feasts and dances are held here as well.

A traditional *yano* is made with materials from the **rain forest**. The walls are made from tree trunks. The tree trunks are tied together with long, rope-like **vines**. The roof is made from palm leaves. Today, some of the Yanomami build modern, square huts. They use factory-made materials given to them by outsiders who come to the forest.

◄ Many Yanomami families live together in a round hut called a *yano*.

Inside the yano

More than 20 families may live inside the *yano*. Each family has its own space. Families sleep in **hammocks** hung up around a fire. The fire is used for cooking and heating. Each family hangs its baskets, containers, and tools from the *yano*'s roof.

◀ In the *yano*, hammocks are strung up one above the other, with the youngest children sleeping at the bottom.

MOVING

Every few years, the *yano* becomes leaky and full of insects. The villagers move out of the old *yano*. They clear another space in the forest. They build a new *yano* and burn down the old house.

Daily Life

In a Yanomami village, men and women traditionally do different jobs. The men hunt animals for food. The women look after the children and do the cooking, as well as collect water from the river and firewood from the forest. Both men and women work on the village gardens.

▸ A garden is cut out of the forest. Pumpkins, sweet potatoes, and cassava (plants with roots that can be eaten) are growing.

▼ A Yanomami man in the village garden digs out some manioc (see page 15) with a knife.

Gardening

Every village has its own "garden." This is a clearing in the forest where people grow crops, such as **plantains** (a type of banana). They also grow sugarcane and sweet potatoes. The women clear away weeds and plant new crops. They collect cotton, which they use to make **hammocks** and clothing.

FAMILY LIFE

A Yanomami family may be made up of a father, mother, and several children. The Yanomami do not have a special **ceremony** when they get married. They simply hang their hammocks next to each other in the *yano*. For the first few years, mothers keep their babies with them while they work. Children sleep with their mother in her hammock until they are about five years old, or until a new baby is born into the family.

13

Yanomami Food

Traditionally, the Yanomami get all the food they need from the **rain forest**. They eat rain forest plants. They hunt rain forest animals for meat. Today, some Yanomami also eat Western food, such as canned food.

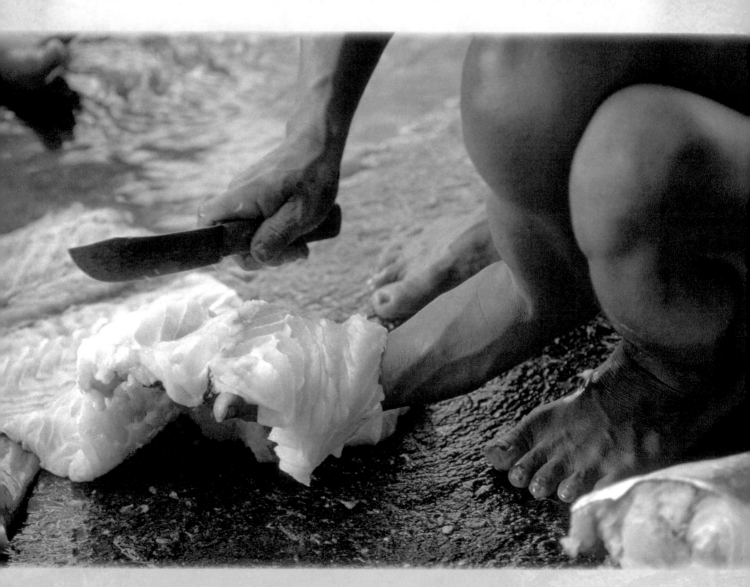

▲ A Yanomami man cuts up a fish that he has caught in the river.

MANIOC BREAD

Manioc is a vegetable. It looks like a long potato. If it is not prepared properly, it can be poisonous. Manioc is a very important part of the Yanomami diet. It is made into bread. The manioc is peeled and grated. The poisonous juice is squeezed out. The paste that is left is made into thick, flat cakes. These are left in the sun to dry. Then, the cakes are baked over the fire.

▶ A Yanomami woman grates manioc, which she will make into bread.

Traditional food

The Yanomami grow a wide range of fruits and vegetables in their gardens. They eat **plantains** at many meals. They boil or roast them. Sometimes they mash them up with water to make a drink. The Yanomami collect many plants that grow wild in the forest, including peach palm fruits. They also collect Brazil nuts, pineapples, and avocados. They catch fish in the river, using baskets or poisoned arrows.

Going Hunting

The Yanomami hunt **rain forest** animals, such as **tapirs** (see opposite), for their meat. Tapirs are large, pig-like animals. The Yanomami also hunt monkeys, giant anteaters, and wild pigs. It is very important for Yanomami men to be good hunters. They earn respect by bringing back meat for their families.

A hunt sets off

The hunters leave the village early in the morning. They walk through the forest, following animal **tracks**. They have to be highly skilled. Many rain forest animals hide during the daytime. The hunters use whistles and hand signals to speak to each other. They do not want to scare away the animals.

▶ This Yanomami boy is practicing with his bow and arrow to become a good hunter.

▲ Tapirs, like this one, are hunted by the Yanomami for their meat.

BEING A HUNTER

The hunters never say the names of the animals they hunt. They believe that it will make the animals disappear. Instead, they may call the animal they hunt a "warrior." Traditionally, they kill the animals with bows and arrows. The arrows are dipped in poison made from the bark of a rain forest tree. Today, the Yanomami also use shotguns. Back in the *yano*, the hunters share the meat with the other families. Hunters never eat meat from animals that they have killed themselves.

Clothes and Dressing Up

The weather is warm and sticky in the **rain forest**. The Yanomami do not need to wear many clothes. Traditionally, both men and women are naked or wear cotton **loincloths**. Loincloths look like short aprons. Today, some Yanomami also wear Western-style clothes, such as T-shirts. They might also wear shorts and dresses. They get these clothes from outsiders.

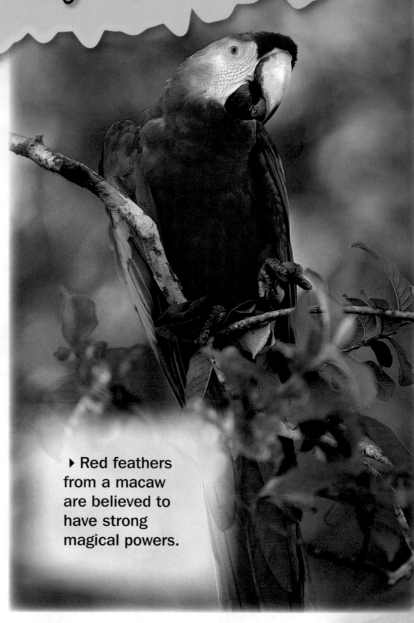

▶ Red feathers from a macaw are believed to have strong magical powers.

Dressing up

Yanomami men and women like to wear jewelry. The jewelry is made from forest materials. They make necklaces from strings of seeds or animal teeth. They pierce their ears and wear flowers or feathers as earrings. They also pierce their noses and lower lips. They put short, thin sticks through the holes.

BODY PAINTING

The Yanomami like to paint their faces and bodies for feasts and other celebrations. They use red and black patterns. These patterns are based on rain forest plants and animals. The red and black paints are made from crushed seeds. The paint can also be made from the fruits of rain forest trees.

On special occasions, men like to wear feather headdresses and armbands. The feathers come from rain forest birds, such as macaws. They might also get feathers from parrots and toucans. The Yanomami believe that the feathers give them special powers and protect them from evil **spirits**.

◀ A Yanomami man has painted his face and body and put on a feather armband. He is ready for a special occasion.

Learning and Leisure

Today, some Yanomami children go to schools run by the government. But most children do not go to school. Instead, they learn useful skills from their parents. They soon know which animals to hunt. They quickly learn which plants to use for food and medicine. They learn about Yanomami history and beliefs by listening to stories.

▲ Yanomami children are taught in an outdoor school in the Amazon **rain forest**.

Growing up

Yanomami boys practice their hunting skills using miniature bows and arrows. They hunt small animals such as lizards. They also hunt frogs and birds. They spend most of the day with their friends, climbing trees and swimming in the river. Girls have less time to play. From an early age, they learn how to cook and make **hammocks**. They also help to look after the younger children.

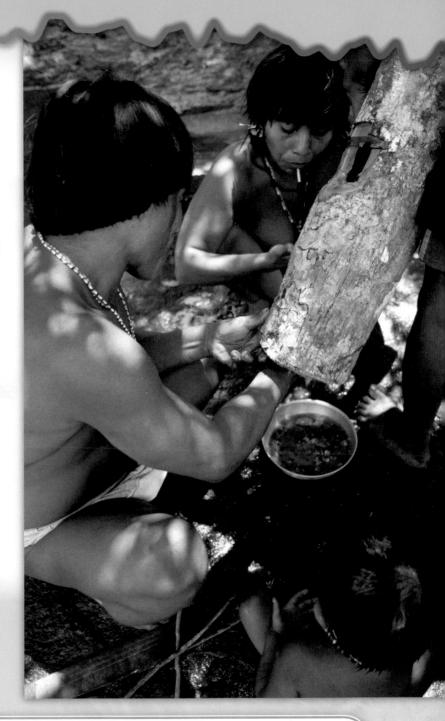

▶ These Yanomami children are learning how to get honey from a bees' nest inside a rain forest tree.

THE STORY OF FIRE

A Yanomami **legend,** or story, says that long ago, the Yanomami did not have fire to cook on. They ate raw food. Then, lightning struck the forest and started a fire. Iwariwa, the **cayman** (an alligator-like animal), swallowed the fire. He kept it inside his body. One day, someone tricked Iwariwa into laughing. He opened his mouth and the fire escaped. That is how the Yanomami discovered fire.

Yanomami Beliefs

The Yanomami believe that all living things have powerful **spirits**. The spirits live in *yanos* in the sky. The spirits often come down to Earth. They can be helpful or harmful. They can cure people who are sick. They can help hunters find animals. They can also cause sickness and bring bad luck.

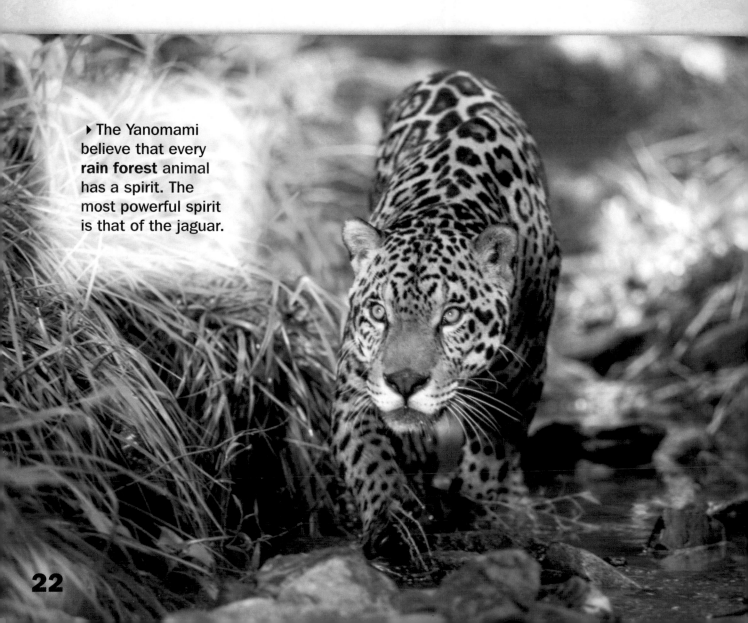

▸ The Yanomami believe that every **rain forest** animal has a spirit. The most powerful spirit is that of the jaguar.

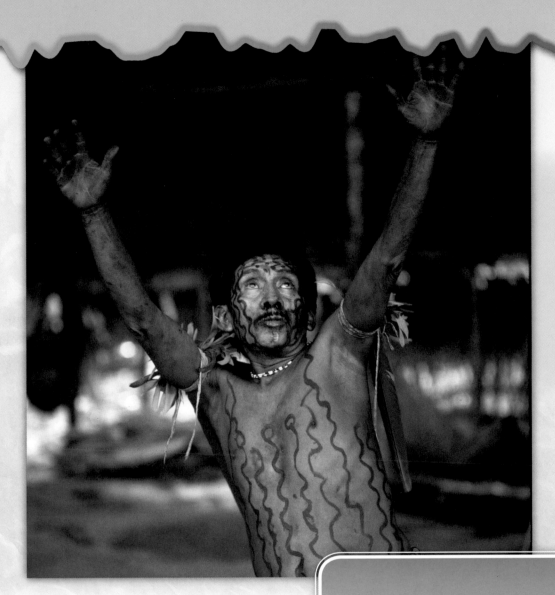

◄ When a shaman talks to an animal spirit, he acts like that animal. He uses animal noises and movements.

Talking to the spirits

The Yanomami believe that **shamans** are the only people who can talk to the spirits. When someone is sick, shamans call to the spirits. They ask a spirit to visit and help the person. Different spirits have different powers.

YANOMAMI UNIVERSE

The Yanomami believe that the **universe** has four layers. Nothing lives in the top layer. This is where the universe began. The next layer down is a beautiful place in the sky. This is where the spirits of dead people go. Below this is the layer containing Earth. The bottom layer is a terrible place. It is where the spirits of people go if they fall from the sky layer.

Ceremonies and Dances

Sometimes the Yanomami invite guests from other villages for a special feast. The space in the middle of the **yano** is cleared for singing and dancing. The women prepare special food. They boil **plantains** and roast meat. Everyone gets dressed up.

◄ Yanomami dancers perform at a feast. Some dances may last for many hours.

Funeral ceremony

A *yaimo* is held when someone dies. This is a special **ceremony**. A *yaimo* may last for several days. The ceremony begins with singing and dancing. There is plenty to eat and drink. An important part of a *yaimo* is trading with people from other villages. Traditionally, the Yanomami do not use money. They **exchange** (swap) goods instead. They might trade an ax and some fish hooks for a new bow and arrow.

▶ These Yanomami are dressed in special costumes, ready to go to a funeral feast.

A FUNERAL CUSTOM

When a Yanomami dies, his or her body is burned on a fire. The ashes are collected and put into hollowed-out **gourds**. At the *yaimo*, the **shaman** mixes the ashes with banana juice. The dead person's family drinks the mixture. The Yanomami believe that the dead person's **spirit** will live on in his or her family.

Under Threat

The Yanomami have lived in the **rain forest** for thousands of years. They have learned how to use the forest without harming it. But today, the forest is being destroyed. This is harming the plants and animals that the Yanomami rely on for food.

▲ These rain forest trees are being cut down and burned to make space for a cattle ranch (a large farm).

YANOMAMI LAND

Many people have tried to help the Yanomami. In 1992 the government of Brazil set aside part of the forest. They called it Yanomami Park. This was for the Yanomami only, and it was somewhere they could live safely. Sadly, some gold miners are still breaking the rules and going into the park.

▶ Gold miners look for gold in the Amazon rain forest. Digging mines like this one is damaging the forest.

Yanomami in danger

Some rain forest **products** are very valuable. In the 1980s, gold was discovered on Yanomami land. This was in Brazil (see map on page 5). Thousands of miners came to the rain forest to dig up the gold and sell it. The miners shot many animals. They poisoned the rivers with **chemicals**. They built roads and damaged huge areas of forest. Many Yanomami were shot. Thousands more Yanomami died from diseases, such as the flu and measles. They caught these illnesses from the gold miners.

Could You Be a Yanomami?

Take this quiz. Could you live in the **rain forest** like the Yanomami?

1. What does the name "Yanomami" mean?
A) Human being B) Little person C) Tall person

2. Which huge river runs through the Amazon rain forest?
A) Mississippi B) Amazon C) Nile

3. What do the Yanomami call the rain forest?
A) **Yano** B) *Urihi* C) *Nano*

4. Which rain forest plants would you get water from?
A) Bromeliad B) **Vine** C) Water lily

5. What do the Yanomami live in?
A) Tent B) Castle C) *Yano*

6. Which crop might you find in a Yanomami's garden?
A) **Plantain** B) Potatoes C) Rice

7. Which animals do the Yanomami hunt?
A) Cow B) **Tapir** C) Dinosaurs

8. Which bird's red feathers are very special?
A) A macaw's B) A sparrow's C) A hummingbird's

9. Which animal might you meet in the Amazon rain forest?
A) Giraffe B) Jaguar C) Polar bear

10. Whom do the Yanomami go to when they are sick?
A) **Shaman** B) Friend C) Nurse

QUIZ ANSWERS:
6A; 7B; 8A; 9B; 10A;
1A; 2B; 3B; 4A; 5C;

Find Out for Yourself

Books to read

Aloian, Molly, and Bobbie Kalman. *Amazon River Habitat*. New York: Crabtree, 2007.

Pyers, Greg. *Rain Forest Explorer* (*Habitat Explorer* series). Chicago: Raintree, 2005.

Thompson, Gare. *Amazon Journey: Cruising the Rain Forest*. Washington, D.C.: National Geographic, 2006.

Websites

www.survival-international.org
The website of Survival International, an organization that helps threatened people around the world protect their way of life.

www.rain forestfoundation.org
The website of the Rain forest Foundation, an organization that helps protect the environment and way of life of rain forest people.

www.ran.org
The Rain forest Action Network's website—RAN works to save the rain forests and protect the lives of rain forest people.

www.socioambiental.org/e/
A detailed guide to the rain forest people of Brazil.

Disclaimer
All the Internet addresses (URLs) given in this book were valid at the time of going to press. However, due to the dynamic nature of the Internet, some addresses may have changed, or sites may have ceased to exist since publication. While the author and publishers regret any inconvenience this may cause readers, no responsibility for any such changes can be accepted by either the author or the publishers. It is recommended that adults supervise children on the Internet.

Glossary

cayman animal related to alligators and crocodiles

ceremony public celebration

chemical strong substance used in making and cleaning things

climate type of weather a place has over a long time

culture group of people with a particular way of life

equator imaginary line around Earth. The places along the equator have hot weather all year round.

exchange swap something for something else

gourd fruit with a hard shell. When the fruit is taken out, the shells are dried and used as drinking cups and containers.

hammock long piece of cotton cloth, which is hung up by both ends and used as a bed

legend ancient, traditional story

loincloth short piece of cloth that is worn around a person's waist

plantain banana-like fruit

product object that is made or grown

rain forest thick, green forest that grows around the equator

shaman person who communicates with the spirit world and calls on the spirits to heal sick people

spirit invisible force inside people and other living things

tapir large, pig-like animal that lives in the rain forest

track footprint or mark left by an animal in the rain forest soil

universe another name for the world and everything around it

vine long, woody root of a rain forest plant, which grows high up on the tree branches

yaimo Yanomami funeral ceremony

yano round hut where many Yanomami families live together

Index